CW01280965

LET'S LOOK AT VOLCANOES

Graham Rickard

Language Consultant
Diana Bentley
University of Reading

Artist
Carolyn Scrace

Wayland

Let's Look At

Aircraft	Outer Space
Big Cats	Rain
Bikes	The Seasons
Castles	Sharks
Circuses	Sunshine
Colours	Tractors
Dinosaurs	Trucks
Farming	Trains
Horses	Volcanoes

Editor: Sarah Doughty

First published in 1989 by
Wayland (Publishers) Ltd
61, Western Road, Hove
East Sussex, BN3 1JD, England

© Copyright 1989 Wayland (Publishers) Ltd

British Library Cataloguing in Publication Data
Rickard, Graham
 Let's look at volcanoes.
 1. Volcanoes – For children
 I. Title   II. Scrace, Carolyn
 551.2′1

 ISBN 1-85210-486-4

Phototypeset by Kalligraphics, Horley, Surrey
Printed and bound by Casterman, S.A., Belgium

Words printed in **bold** are explained in the glossary.

Contents

Changes below the earth 4
Different types of volcanoes 6
Where volcanoes are found 8
Volcanoes long ago 10
Krakatoa erupts 12
Volcanoes today 14
Escape from Tristan da Cunha 16
The effects of volcanoes 18
Giant waves 20
Hot springs 22
Measuring volcanoes 24
Protection from volcanoes 26
Stories about volcanoes 28

Glossary 30
Books to read 31
Index 32

Changes below the earth

Far below the earth and sea, enormous changes have taken place, over millions of years. Underneath the outer layer or **crust** of the earth, rocks have slowly changed and moved. In some places this has caused large pieces of crust to rub against each other and form mountains and seas.

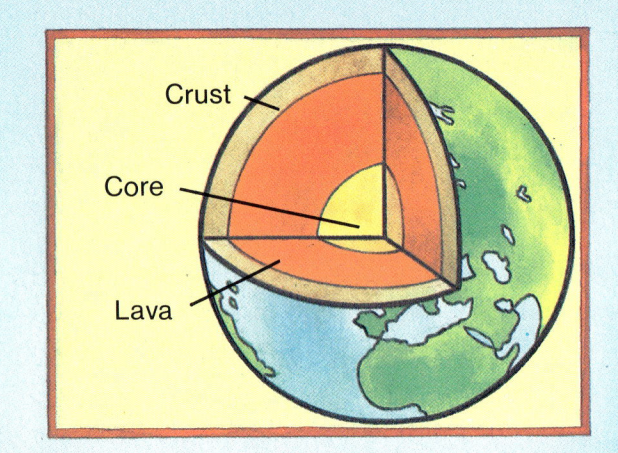

Crust
Core
Lava

Mountains

Crust

Molten lava

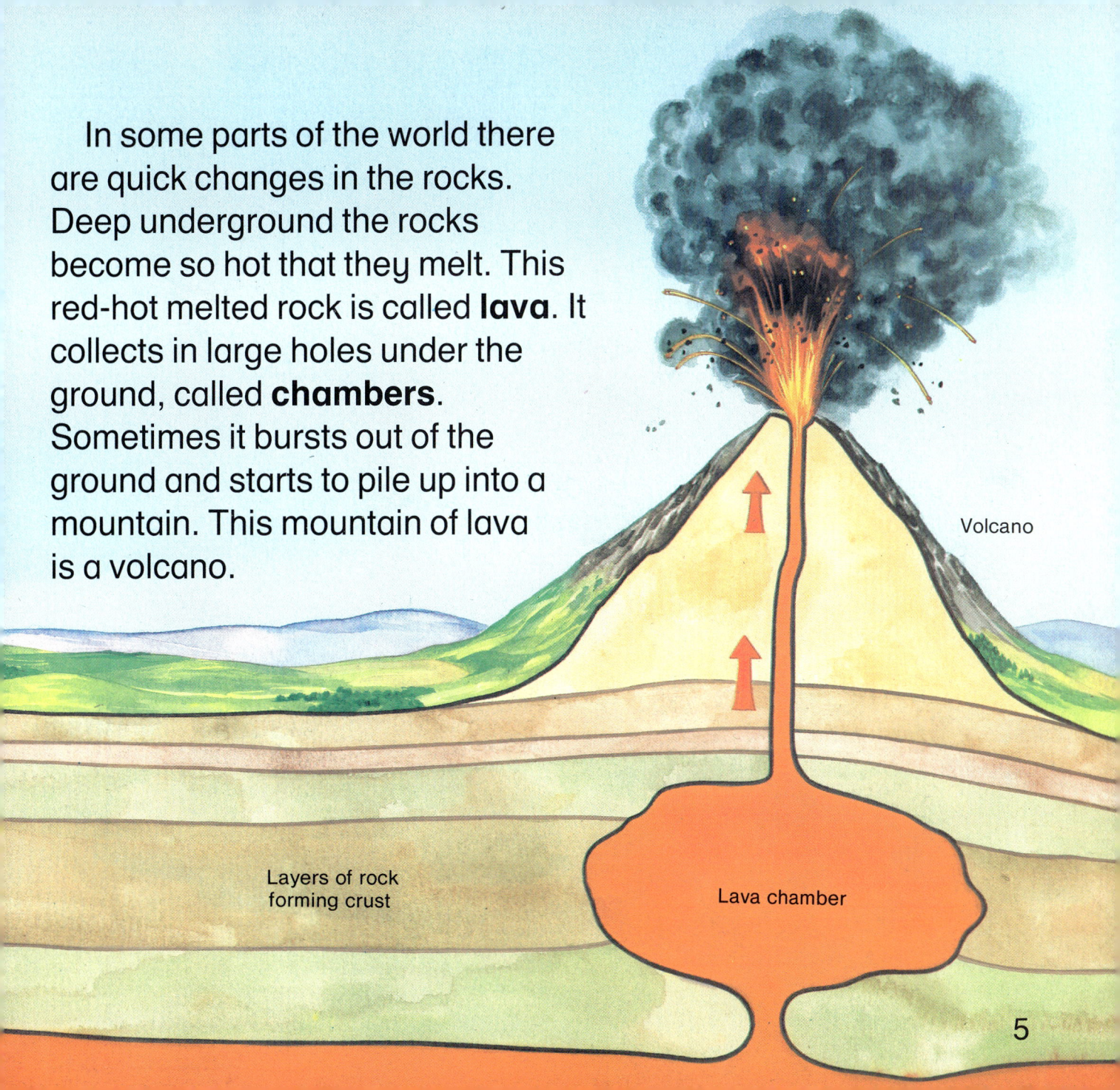

In some parts of the world there are quick changes in the rocks. Deep underground the rocks become so hot that they melt. This red-hot melted rock is called **lava**. It collects in large holes under the ground, called **chambers**. Sometimes it bursts out of the ground and starts to pile up into a mountain. This mountain of lava is a volcano.

Volcano

Layers of rock forming crust

Lava chamber

Different types of volcanoes

Many volcanoes explode with such force, that they shoot lava and rocks high into the air. They are forced out of a **crater** at the top of the **cone.** Rivers of burning lava pour out of the volcano. The lava is sticky and hardens very quickly.

Crust

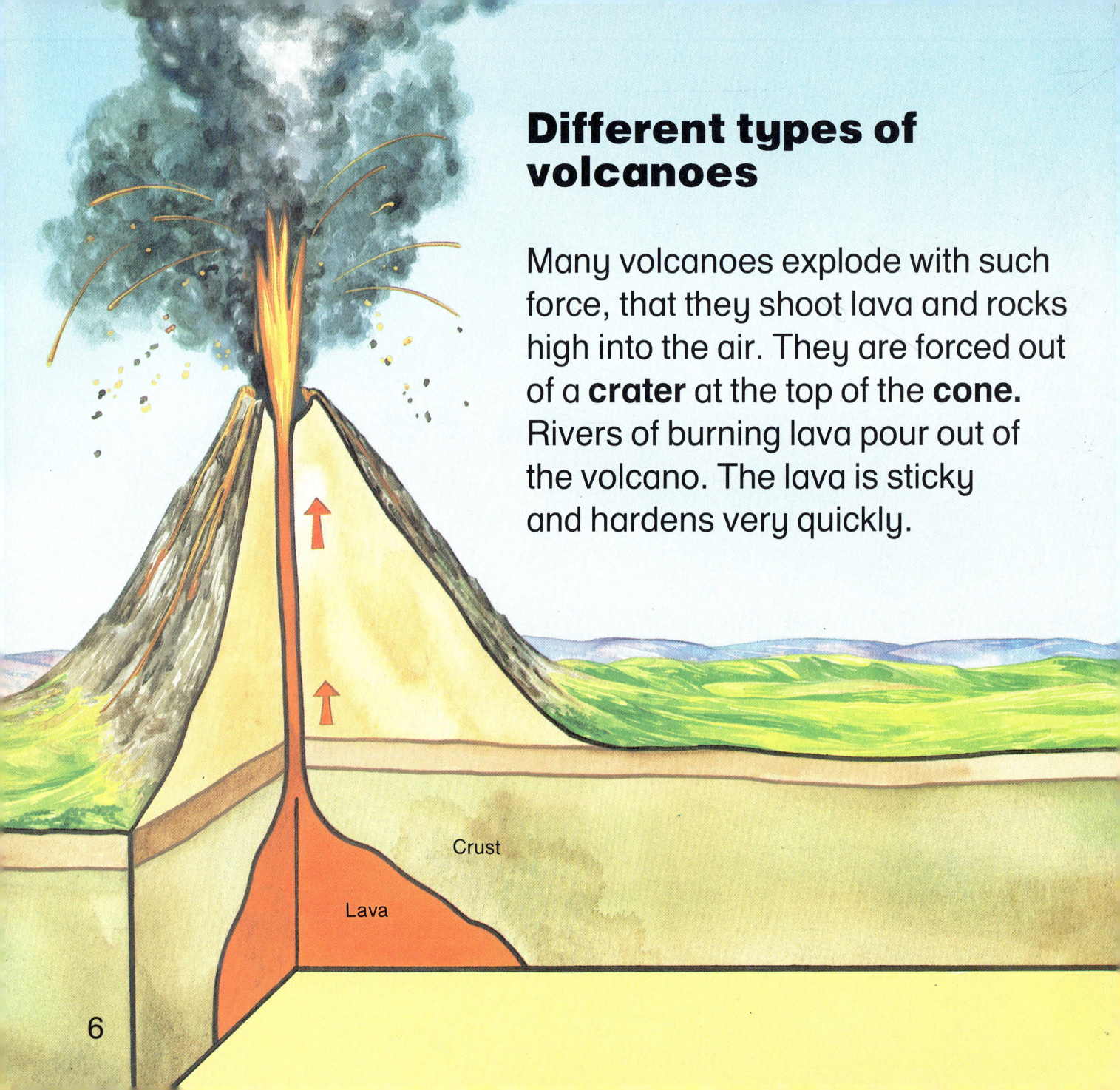

Lava

Other volcanoes are much quieter. Sometimes very runny lava pours out of long cracks in the ground. It flows a long way before it cools and hardens to form large areas of flat rock. Sometimes the lava cannot escape and collects in huge lakes of bubbling liquid rock.

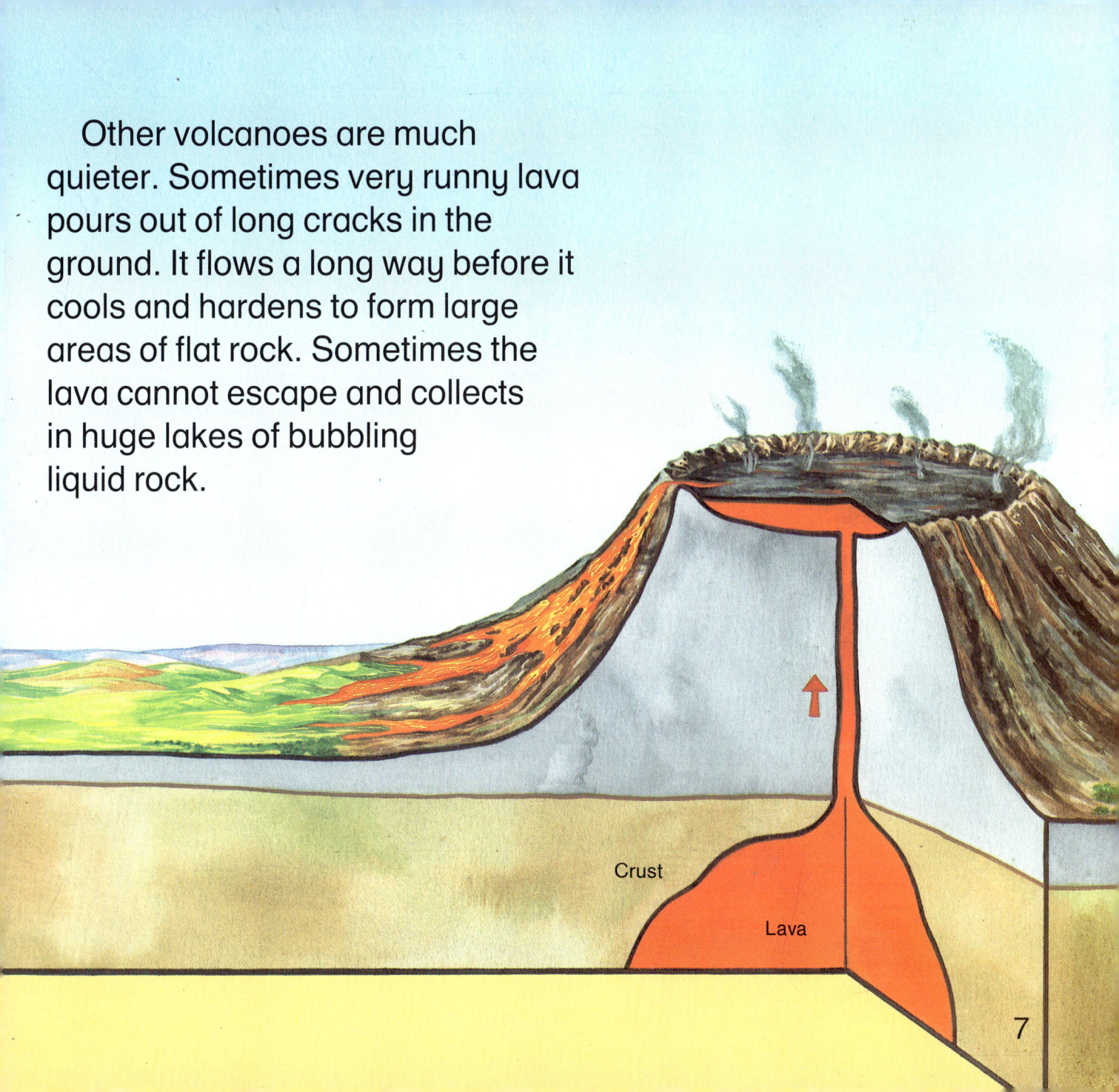

Crust

Lava

Where volcanoes are found

Volcanoes are found in many parts of the world. They often occur together, in groups or long lines. These groups are places where there are cracks in the earth's crust, or where two pieces of crust meet.

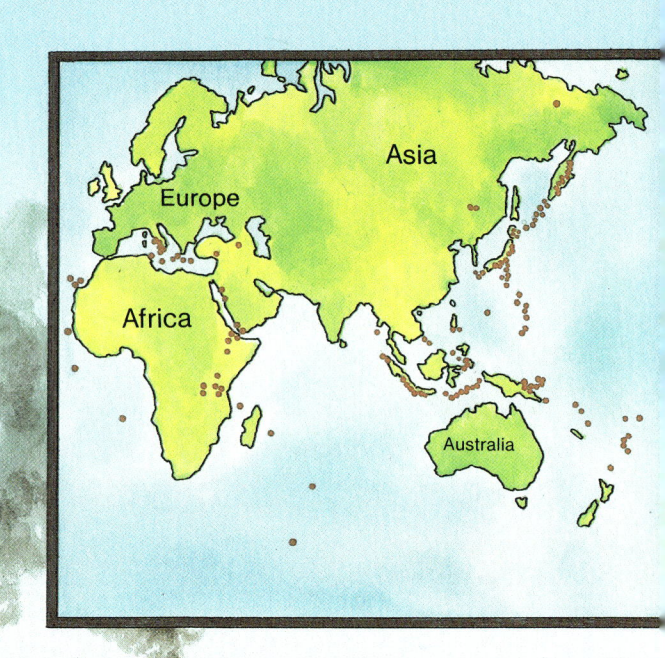

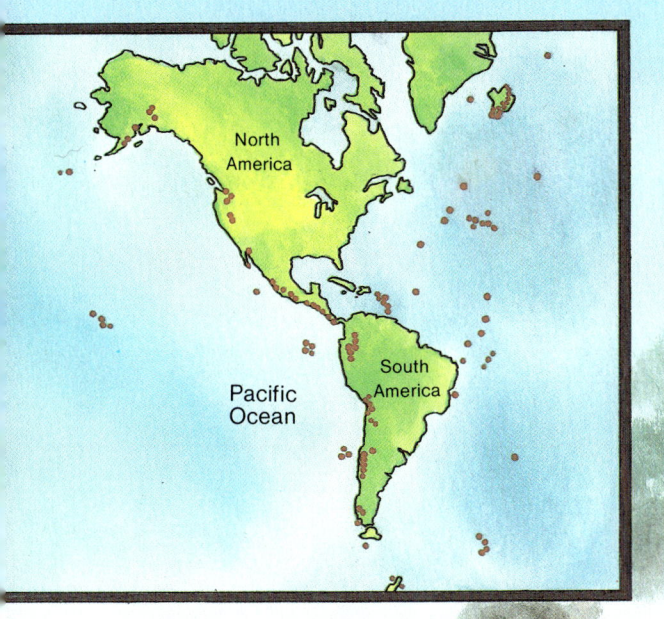

Geologists have been able to find weak spots in the earth's crust. So they know where volcanoes are likely to occur. Altogether we know about 500 **active** volcanoes. There are many volcanoes in the Pacific Ocean. There are also volcanoes in **Antarctica**, South America and New Zealand.

1. The dormant volcano

2. The volcano erupts

3. After the explosion

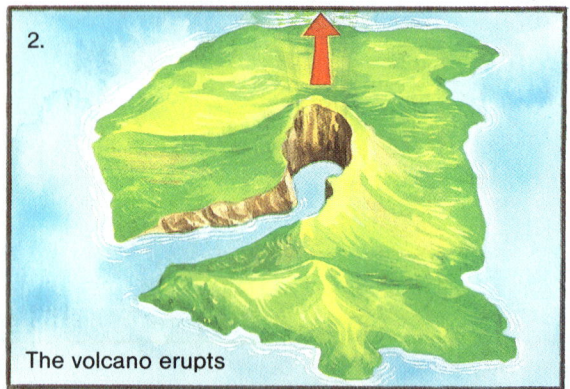

Volcanoes long ago

Long ago, the island of Santorini in Greece was a high volcanic cone. It had not erupted for a long time so people thought it was **dormant**. Many people lived on the island, but in 1470 BC the volcano started to **erupt** and so many people left. Soon after there was an enormous explosion and the whole island blew up into pieces and fell into the sea. Today there are several islands, formed from the eruption.

Santorini islands today

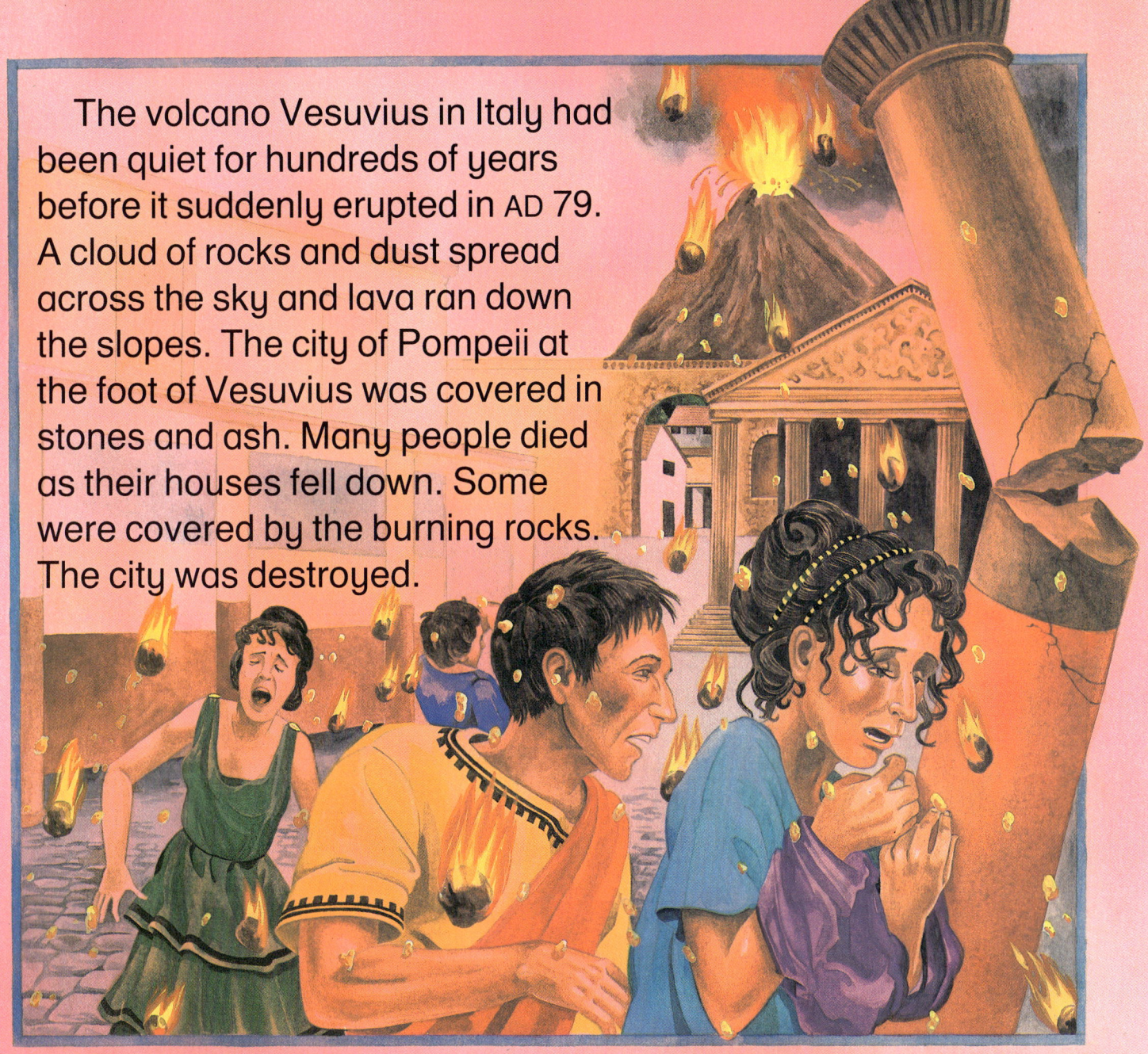

The volcano Vesuvius in Italy had been quiet for hundreds of years before it suddenly erupted in AD 79. A cloud of rocks and dust spread across the sky and lava ran down the slopes. The city of Pompeii at the foot of Vesuvius was covered in stones and ash. Many people died as their houses fell down. Some were covered by the burning rocks. The city was destroyed.

Krakatoa erupts

Many people lived on the island of Krakatoa in Indonesia. They did not know their home was built on a volcano! In 1883 it started to erupt. For weeks there were small eruptions but they soon faded away. One afternoon a bigger explosion shook the island. Many frightened people fled the island in boats.

The next morning a terrible blast blew the island apart. It destroyed the land and every person left on shore. A cloud of dust and rock was thrown up in the air blotting out the sun. A large part of the island sank beneath the sea. The noise of the explosion could be heard thousands of kilometres away.

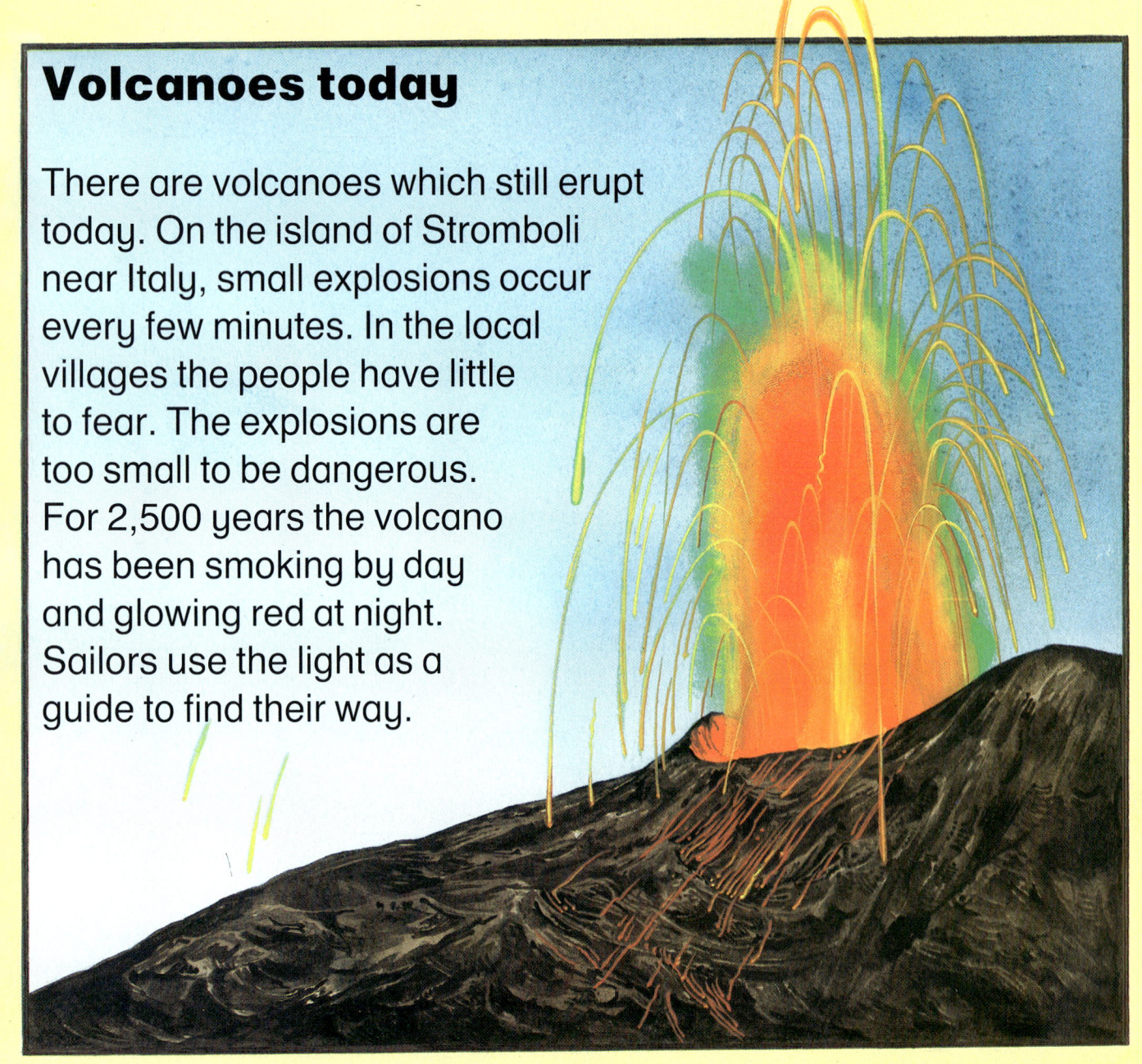

Volcanoes today

There are volcanoes which still erupt today. On the island of Stromboli near Italy, small explosions occur every few minutes. In the local villages the people have little to fear. The explosions are too small to be dangerous. For 2,500 years the volcano has been smoking by day and glowing red at night. Sailors use the light as a guide to find their way.

Some volcanoes today can still be very dangerous. In 1980 Mount St Helens in the USA started to swell up. Then a huge explosion blew off the side of the mountain, killing all the animals, fish and trees that lived there. Luckily very few people died. Today a large area is covered with a thick layer of ash and dust, and no plants can grow there now.

Mount St Helens before the explosion

Escape from Tristan da Cunha

Martha was a little girl who lived on an island in the middle of the Atlantic Ocean called Tristan da Cunha. There was an **extinct** volcano on the island. No one thought this would erupt but one day in 1961 Martha was out walking looking for her father's sheep when the ground in front of her suddenly split open. It made a terrible cracking sound. The cracks opened and closed and sheep fell into them. Terrified, Martha ran back home.

Everyone was staring in alarm at the volcano. Boiling hot lava was running down from the top of the volcano into the sea, where it hissed and steamed as it touched the water. Everyone escaped in a small fishing boat, and stayed away until the volcano died down.

The effects of volcanoes

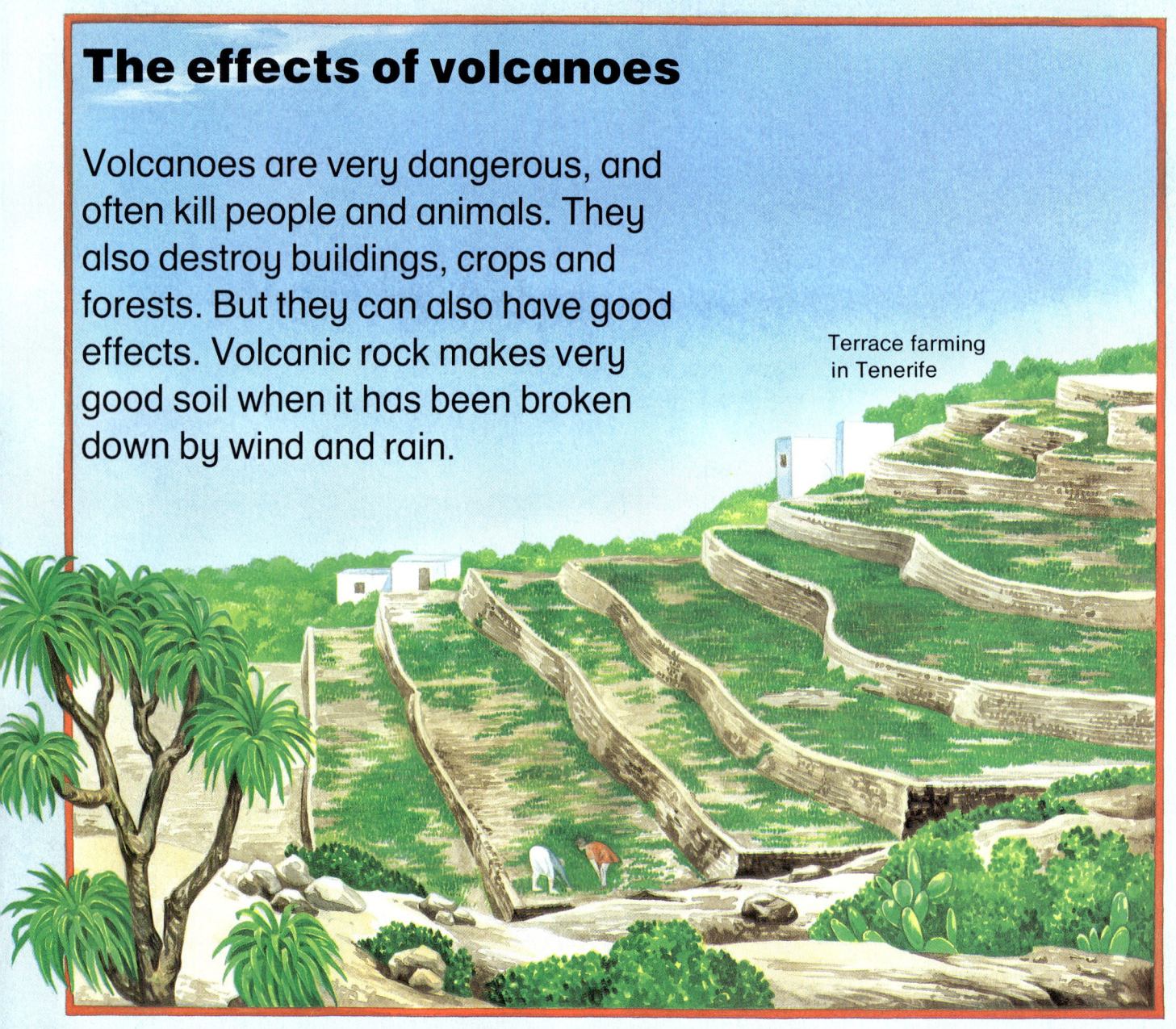

Volcanoes are very dangerous, and often kill people and animals. They also destroy buildings, crops and forests. But they can also have good effects. Volcanic rock makes very good soil when it has been broken down by wind and rain.

Terrace farming in Tenerife

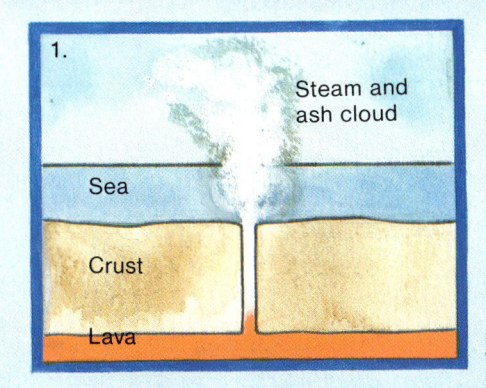

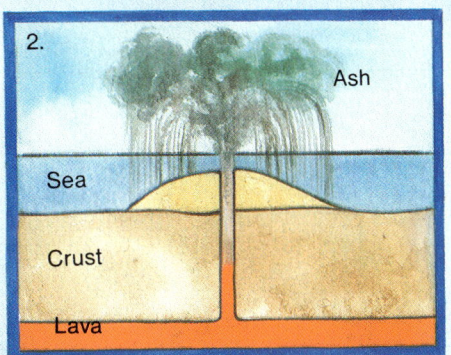

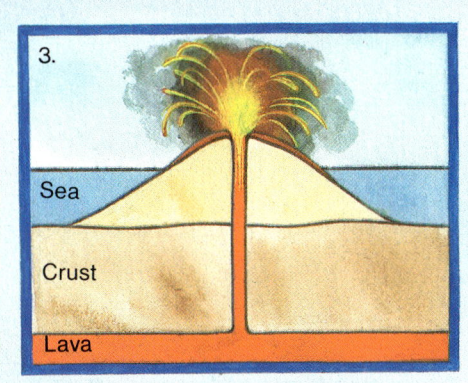

1. Steam and ash cloud
Sea
Crust
Lava

2. Ash
Sea
Crust
Lava

3. Sea
Crust
Lava

4. Island of Surtsey

A few years ago a volcano blew up under the sea near Iceland. At first ash and steam rose upwards. Then material built up on the sea floor until it appeared above sea level. The lava began to flow and small explosions occurred. It formed an island called Surtsey. When the fire and smoke stopped, plants and birds started to live there.

Giant waves

When volcanoes erupt near the sea they often also cause giant waves. These waves are called **tsunami**. In deep water these big waves look small, but they grow into an enormous wall of water as they come near to the coast. The waves crash across the land destroying everything in their path. Crops are destroyed because they are covered with mud.

Tsunami can travel very quickly over very long distances. The giant wave caused by the eruption of Krakatoa took only two days to travel around the earth. Thousands of people were killed in its path.

Hot springs

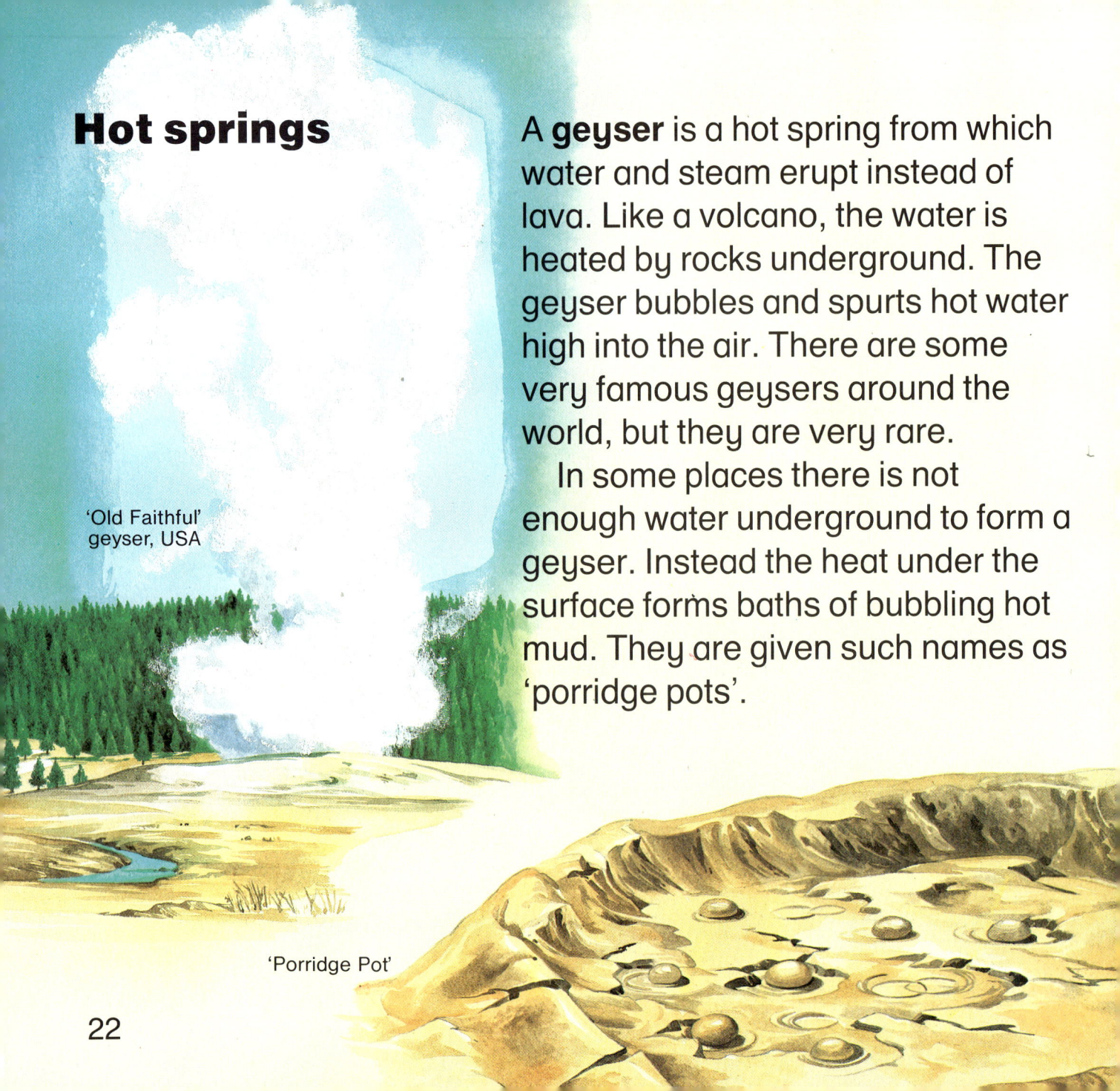

'Old Faithful' geyser, USA

A **geyser** is a hot spring from which water and steam erupt instead of lava. Like a volcano, the water is heated by rocks underground. The geyser bubbles and spurts hot water high into the air. There are some very famous geysers around the world, but they are very rare.

In some places there is not enough water underground to form a geyser. Instead the heat under the surface forms baths of bubbling hot mud. They are given such names as 'porridge pots'.

'Porridge Pot'

Hot springs or geysers can be useful to people. They are sometimes used to heat homes and factories. Steam and gases escape from other holes in the ground. These are called **fumaroles**. These children in Japan are cooking eggs in the hot water from a fumarole.

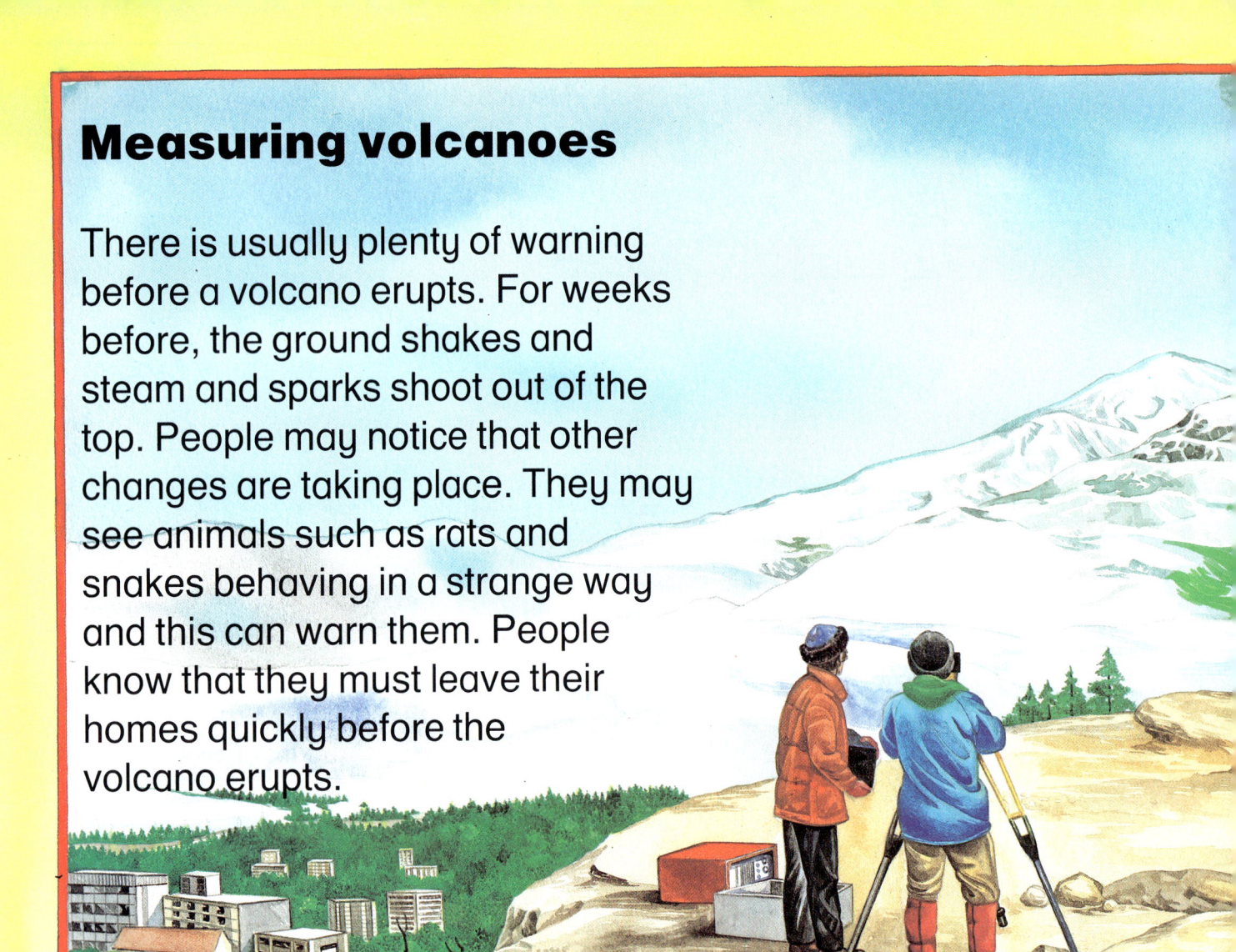

Measuring volcanoes

There is usually plenty of warning before a volcano erupts. For weeks before, the ground shakes and steam and sparks shoot out of the top. People may notice that other changes are taking place. They may see animals such as rats and snakes behaving in a strange way and this can warn them. People know that they must leave their homes quickly before the volcano erupts.

Scientists who study volcanoes help to warn people when an eruption is going to happen. They use special instruments to measure the earth's movements, and to find out if there are any unusual gases in the air. They study pictures from **satellites** in space which give warnings of important changes.

Protection from volcanoes

In many parts of the world, towns and cities are often very close to volcanoes. Volcanoes often erupt suddenly. In 1973 on the island of Heimaey, off the south coast of Iceland, an extinct volcano suddenly erupted. Ash and lava fell onto the town and set fire to the trees and houses. The people had to flee the island for protection.

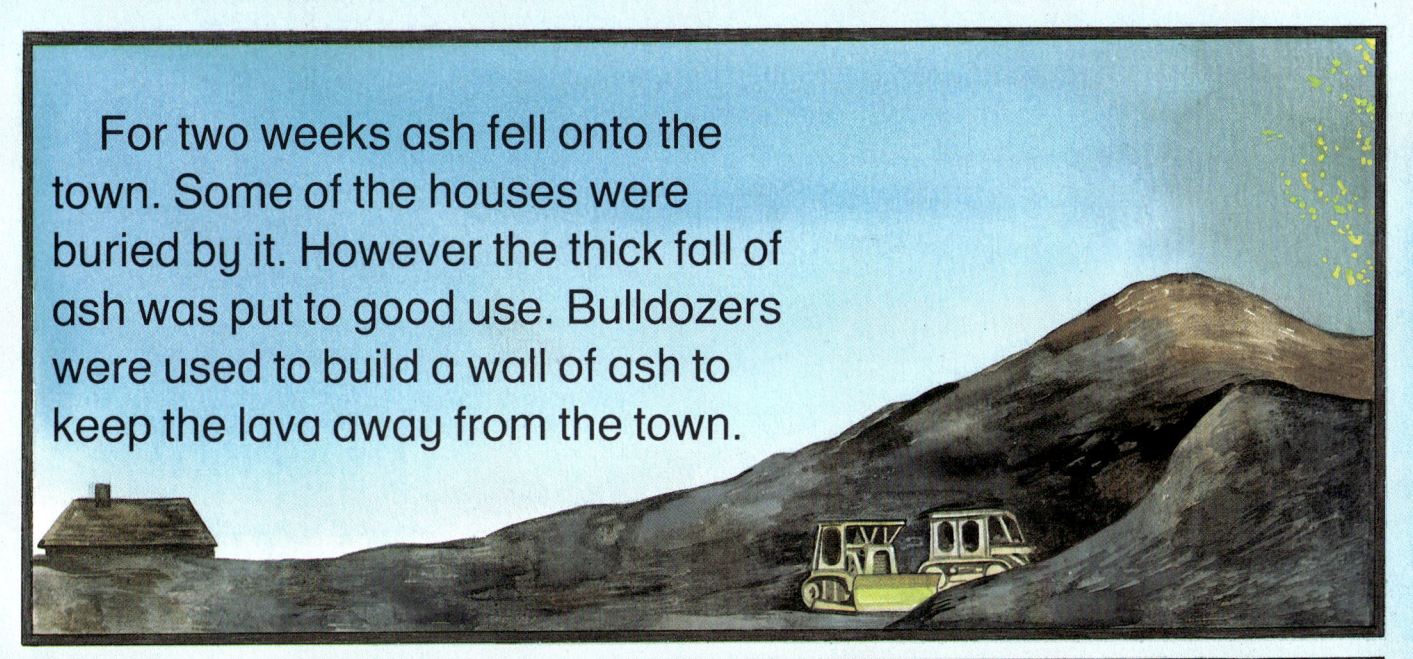

For two weeks ash fell onto the town. Some of the houses were buried by it. However the thick fall of ash was put to good use. Bulldozers were used to build a wall of ash to keep the lava away from the town.

Also, lots of water was sprayed on to the lava to cool it down and slow down its flow.

Stories about volcanoes

In every country where volcanoes are found there have been stories and legends about them.

The word volcano comes from Vulcan who was the Roman god of fire. In many places, people think their gods are angry when a volcano erupts. In the USA, there is an ancient legend about a man who stole fire from a volcano and ran home with it. On the way he tripped and fell, and set the whole world alight.

In Hawaii, people tell the story of Madam Pele, a fire goddess. The story says that she and her family are dancing when the volcano erupts. The lava in Hawaii is called 'Pele's hair'.

Glossary

Active An active volcano is one which still erupts.
Antarctica The very cold area around the South Pole.
Chamber A large hole or cave beneath the earth.
Cone A solid shape that is round at the bottom and pointed at the top.
Crater The large hole at the top of a volcano.
Crust The cool rock on the earth's surface.
Dormant A volcano that has not erupted for a long time.
Erupt To explode and throw out lava.
Extinct A dead volcano that has stopped erupting.
Fumarole A place where gases and steam escape from holes in the ground.
Geologist A person who studies the rocks that form the earth.
Geyser A place where water shoots high in the air from a hole in the ground.
Lava Rock that is so hot that it has melted.
Satellite A spacecraft that orbits the earth.
Tsunami A large wave caused by a volcano.

Books to read

Earthquakes and Volcanoes by David Lambert (Wayland, 1985)
Earthquakes and Volcanoes by Sara Steel (A & C Black, 1982)
The Great Volcanoes by Gillian Hancock (Kaye & Ward, 1982)
Volcanoes by Rupert Furneaux (Kesterel, 1974)
Volcanoes by William Hirst (Blackwell, 1979)
Volcanoes by David Lambert (Franklin Watts, 1985)

Index

A Antarctica 9

C Chambers 5
Crater 6

E Earth's crust 4, 8, 9

F Fire goddess 29
Fumaroles 23

G Geologists 9
Geyser 22–23
Giant waves 20

H Hawaii 29

I Iceland 19, 26–27

K Krakatoa 12–13, 21

L Lava 5, 6, 7, 11, 17, 19

M Mount St Helens 15

N New Zealand 9

P Pacific Ocean 9
Pompeii 11
Porridge pots 22

R Rocks 4, 5, 11, 13, 18

S Santorini 10
Satellites 25
Scientists 25
Soil 18
South America 9
Stromboli 14
Surtsey 19

T Tristan da Cunha 16–17
Tsunami 20–21

U USA 15, 28

V Vesuvius 11
Vulcan 28